Cellular Biology: Organelles, Structure, Function
Written and Illustrated by: APRIL CHLOE TERRAZAS

Dedicated to my beloved cousin.
A.J. Ripps
(1987-2012)

Cellular Biology: Organelles, Structure, Function. April Chloe Terrazas, BS University of Texas at Austin.
Copyright © 2012 Crazy Brainz, LLC

Visit us on the web! www.Crazy-Brainz.com

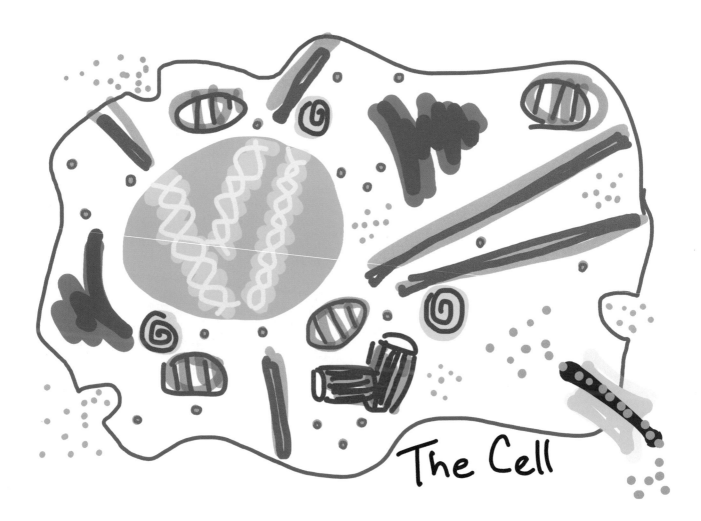

The Cell

This is a cell.

All living things are made of cells.

Cell

There are small parts inside each cell called organelles.

Or-gan-elles

Sound It Out
1. OR
2. GAN
3. LZ

Do you see all of the colored organelles inside the cell?

Turn the page to begin learning about the cell.

You are becoming a cell expert!

Nucleus

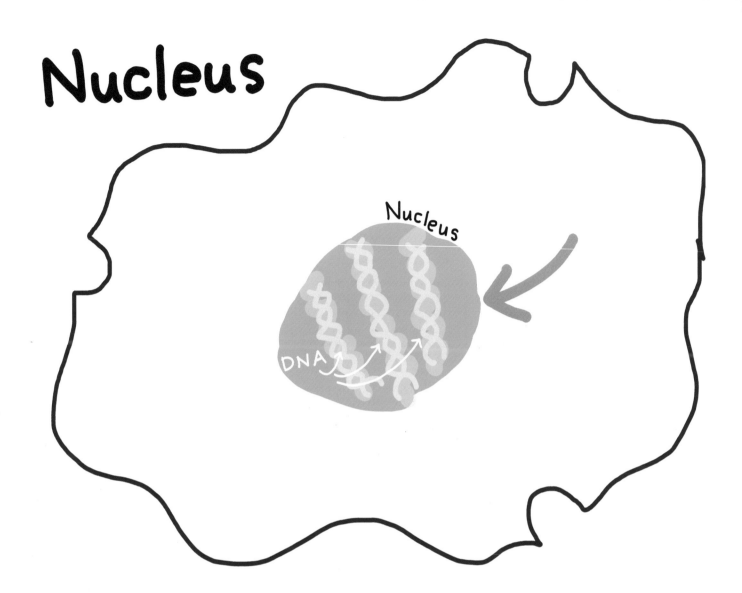

This is the nucleus.

Do you see the yellow lines in the nucleus?

Nu-cle-us

Sound It Out
1. NU
2. KLEE
3. US

DNA is inside the nucleus.

DNA is what makes each person different and special.

The nucleus is like the brain of the cell.

The nucleus controls everything!

Point to the nucleus and the DNA.

How many strands of DNA do you see?

Centrioles

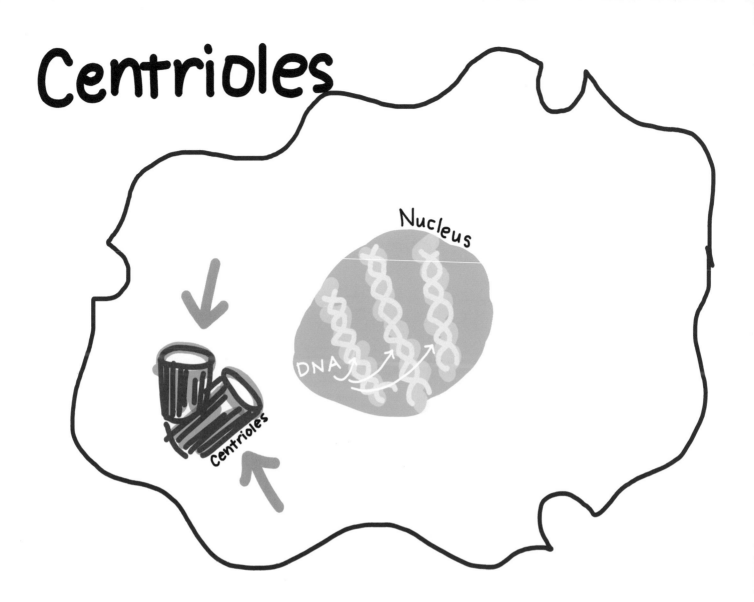

Nucleus

DNA

centrioles

These are centrioles.

Do you see the centrioles next to the nucleus?

Cen-tri-oles

Sound it Out

1. SEN
2. TREE
3. OLS

Centrioles are organelles inside the cell.

Centrioles help the cell make new cells.

Point to the DNA inside the nucleus.

What does the nucleus do?

Microtubules

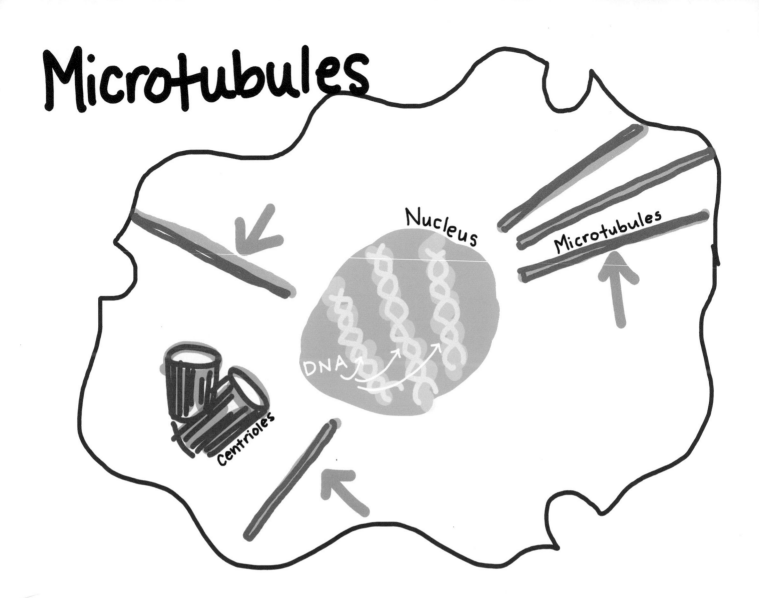

Nucleus

Microtubules

DNA

Centrioles

Mi-cro-tub-ules

These are microtubules.

Microtubules are organelles inside the cell.

Microtubules move things around inside the cell.

Do you see the microtubules?

Can you find the centrioles?

What do the centrioles do?

Where is the nucleus?

Mitochondria

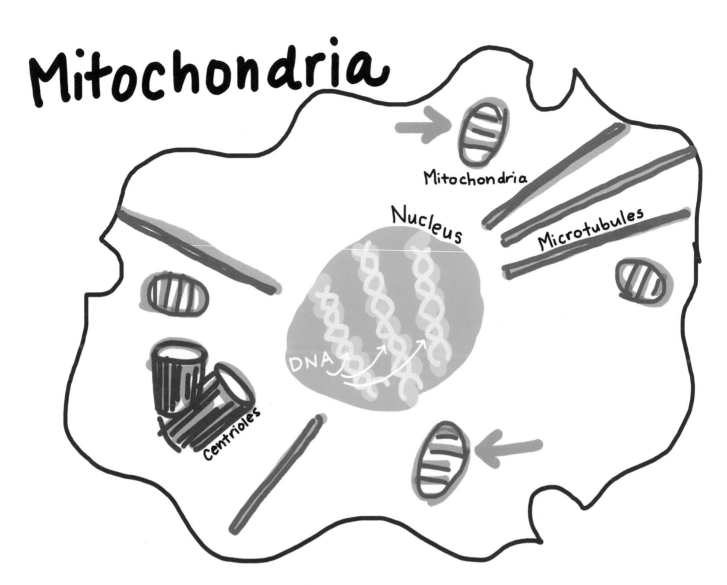

Mitochondria

Nucleus

Microtubules

DNA

Centrioles

Mi-to-chon-dri-a

These are mitochondria.

Mitochondria are organelles inside the cell.

The mitochondria in your cells make energy so you can run and play!

Point to the mitochondria.

Where are the centrioles? Do you see the DNA and nucleus?

What do microtubules do inside the cell?

Lysosomes

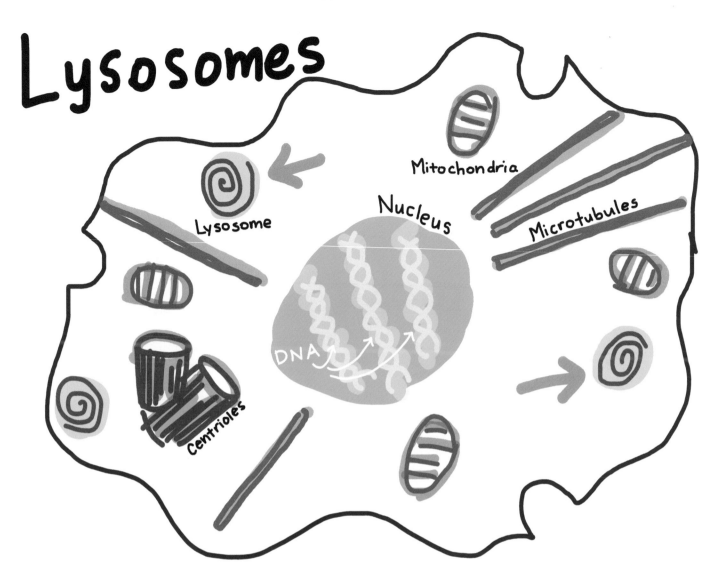

These are **lysosomes**.

Ly-so-somes

Sound It Out

1. LI
2. SO
3. SOMZ

Lysosomes **are** organelles inside the cell.

Lysosomes **are the** trash cans of the cell.

What is inside the nucleus?

What do the mitochondria do inside the cell?

How many lysosomes **do you see?**

Point to the centrioles.

Hormones

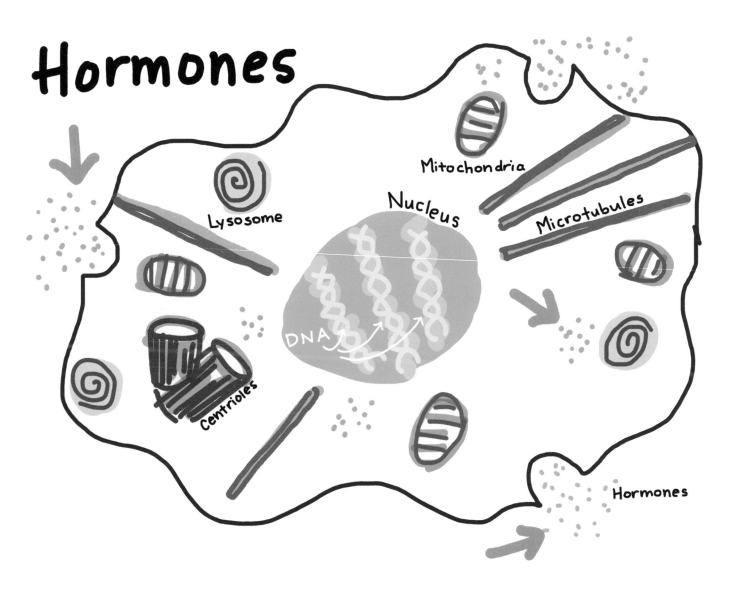

Lysosome

Mitochondria

Nucleus

Microtubules

DNA

Centrioles

Hormones

These are hormones.

Hor-mones

Sound it Out

1. HOR
2. MONZ

Hormones can be inside or outside the cell.

Hormones make you happy!

Do you see the hormones?

Do you see the nucleus with DNA inside?

How many microtubules do you see?

What do the lysosomes do inside the cell?

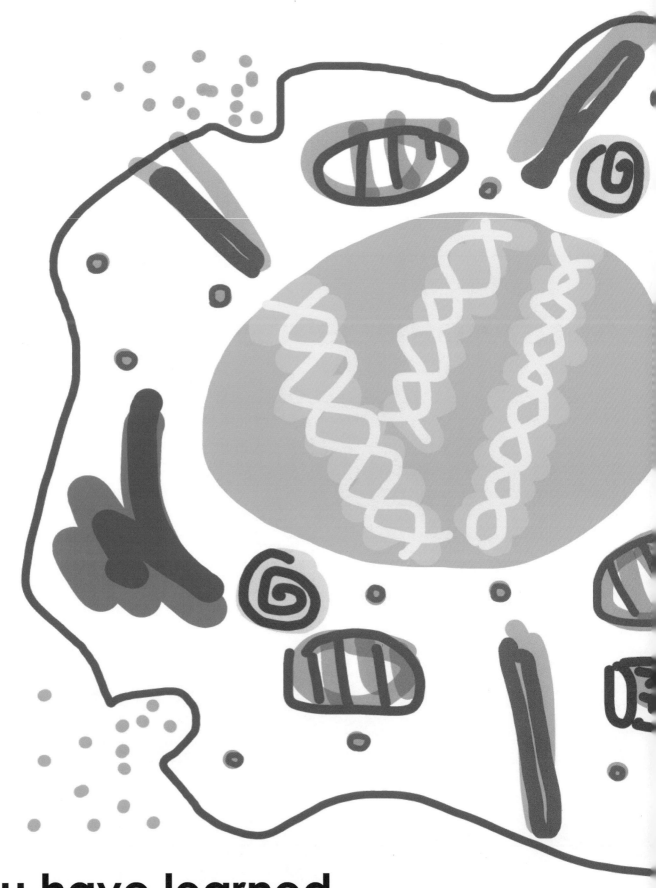

You have learned six parts of the cell...

The Cell

Can you name all six?

Golgi

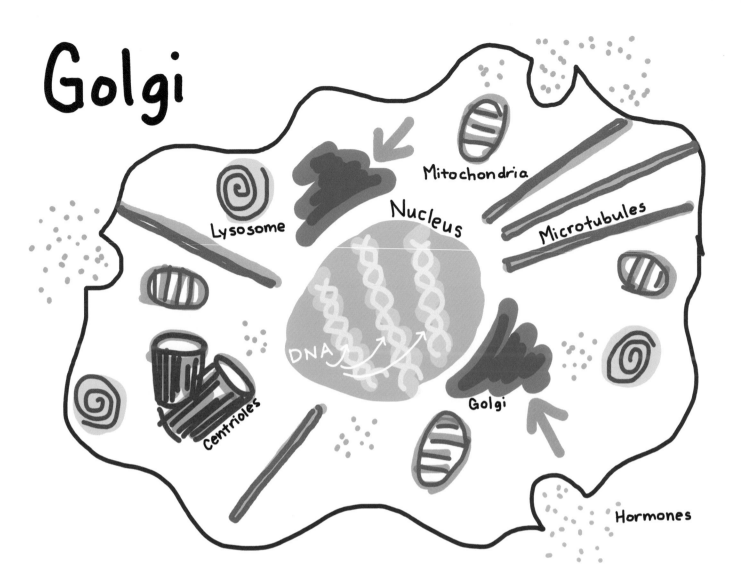

This is the golgi.

Gol-gi

Sound It Out
1. GOL
2. JEE

The **golgi** is an organelle inside the cell.

The **golgi** is made of layers, like pancakes.

The **golgi** makes and sends packages to other parts of the cell, or out of the cell.

 **Do you see the golgi?**

What do the mitochondria do inside the cell?

What is inside the nucleus?

Ribosomes

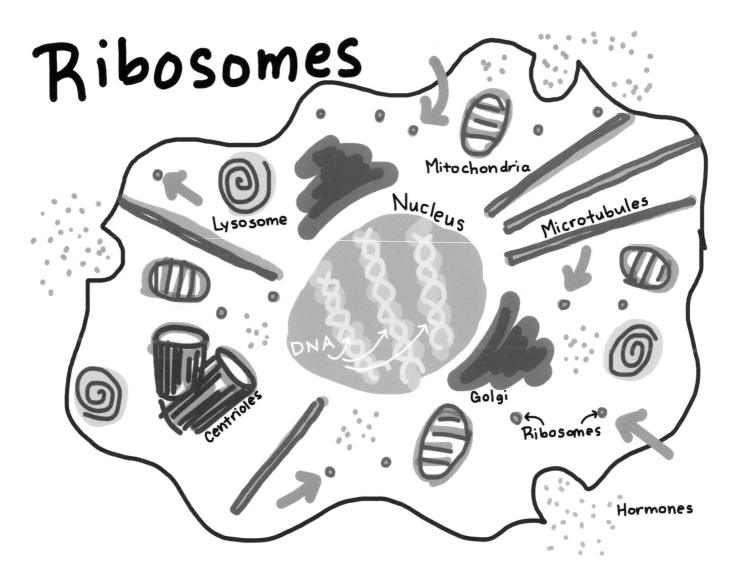

Lysosome
Mitochondria
Nucleus
Microtubules
DNA
Centrioles
Golgi
Ribosomes
Hormones

These are the ribosomes.

Ri-bo-somes

Sound It Out
1. RI
2. BO
3. SOMZ

Ribosomes float around inside the cell.

Ribosomes build proteins.

Where are the mitochondria?

Point to the DNA inside the nucleus.

What does the golgi do inside the cell?

Do you see the microtubules?

Membrane Protein

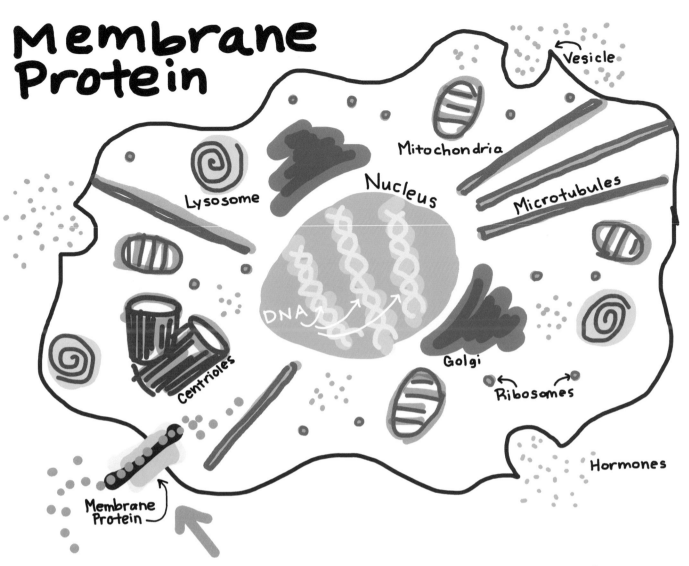

Lysosome, Mitochondria, Nucleus, Vesicle, Microtubules, DNA, Centrioles, Golgi, Ribosomes, Membrane Protein, Hormones

This is a membrane protein.

Mem-brane Pro-tein

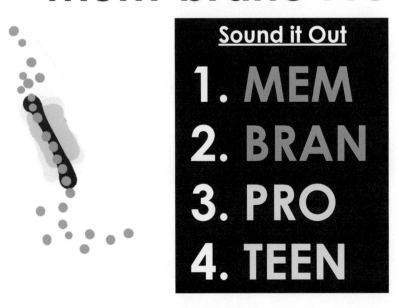

Sound it Out

1. MEM
2. BRAN
3. PRO
4. TEEN

Membrane proteins are stuck in the membrane of the cell.

Membrane proteins move small things in and out of the cell.

Point to the small things moving in and out of the cell.

Where are the centrioles? Do you see the DNA and nucleus?

What do the mitochondria do inside the cell?

Vesicles

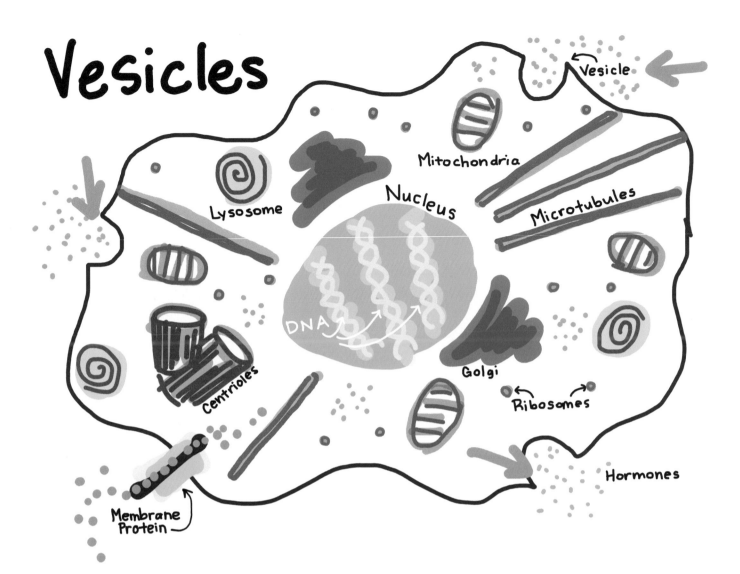

Vesicle

Mitochondria

Nucleus

Microtubules

Lysosome

DNA

Centrioles

Golgi

Ribosomes

Hormones

Membrane Protein

Ves-i-cles

Sound it Out

1. VES
2. EH
3. KLZ

These are vesicles.

Vesicles are little packages. Vesicles carry things like hormones in and out of the cell.

Point to the vesicles carrying hormones in and out of the cell.

Where is the membrane protein?

What do the microtubules do in the cell?

Where is the nucleus and DNA?

Cytoplasm

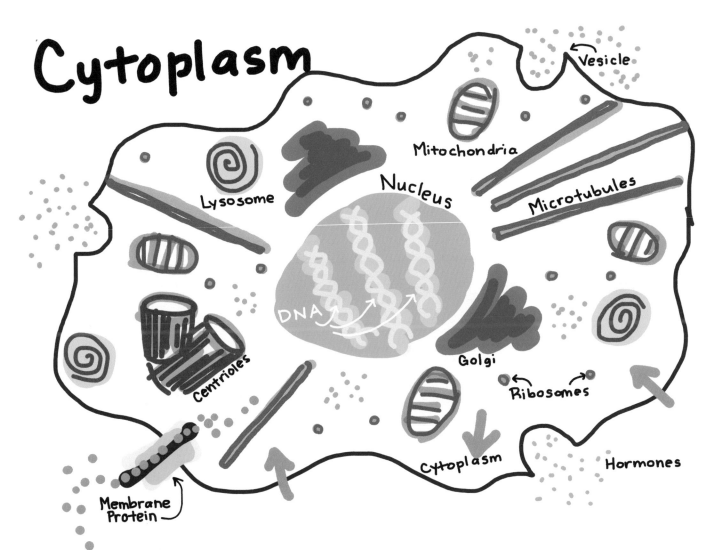

This is the cytoplasm.

Cy-to-plas-m

Sound it Out

1. SI
2. TO
3. PLAZ
4. M

Do you see the open space inside the cell?

This space is filled with cytoplasm.

All of the organelles that you see are floating in cytoplasm inside the cell.

Do you see the centrioles?

Do you know what the golgi does in the cell?

Point to the mitochondria.

Cell Membrane

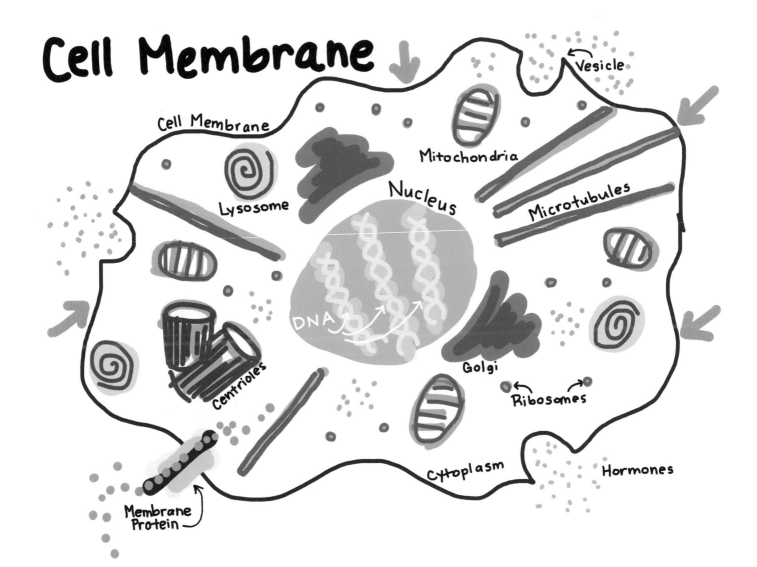

This is the cell membrane.

Cell Mem-brane

Sound it Out
1. SEL
2. MEM
3. BRAN

The cell membrane keeps all of the organelles and cytoplasm together.

Look at everything inside the cell membrane.

Can you point to the centrioles, nucleus,

ribosomes, golgi, hormones, mitochondria, DNA,

microtubules, lysosomes,

vesicles, membrane protein?

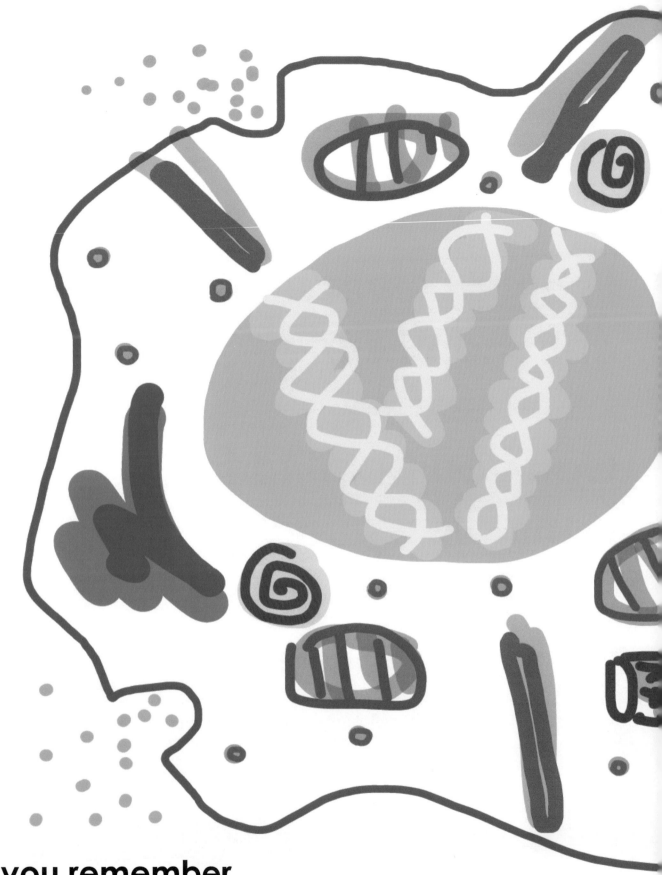

**Do you remember
what each** organelle **does inside the cell?
How many parts of the** cell **can you name?**

The Cell

You are now a Cellular Biology expert!

chemistry:

Coming Spring 2013

the atom and Elements

Ages 0-75

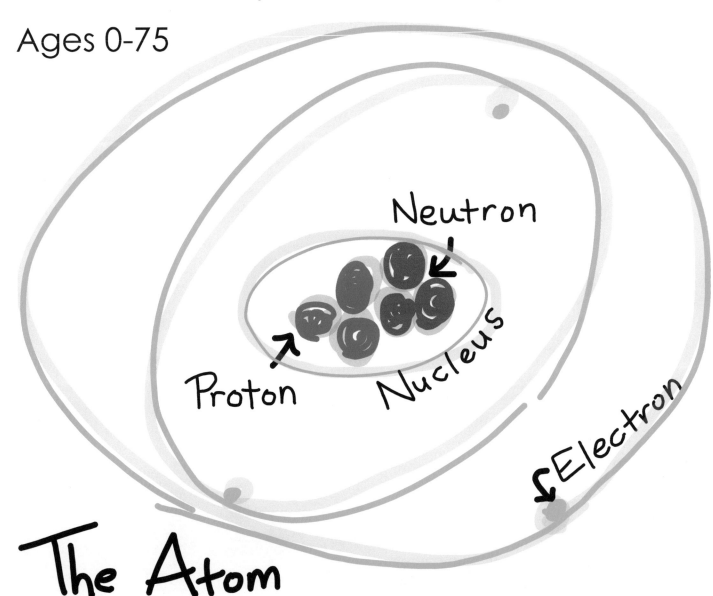

Neutron

Proton

Nucleus

Electron

The Atom

Book two of the
super smart science series™
By: april chloe terrazas

The Cell

You are now a Cellular Biology expert!

chemistry:

Coming Spring 2013

the atom and Elements

Ages 0-75

Neutron

Proton

Nucleus

Electron

The Atom

Book two of the
SUPER SMART SCIENCE SERIES™
By: APRIL CHLOE TERRAZAS

Bold illustrations and **elementary text teach young readers the basics of <u>Cellular Biology</u>.** **Sound-it-out sections** provide aid in pronunciation of organelle names and cell-related words.

A <u>complex topic is made simple</u> to create a solid foundation of science in young minds.

<u>**COMING SOON in the Super Smart Science Series!**</u>
Chemistry: The Atom and Elements
Neurology: The Amazing Central Nervous System
Astronomy: The Solar System...and more!

SUPER SMART SCIENCE SERIES™

$10.⁹⁹

ISBN 978-0-9843848-3-9
5109 9

9 780984 384839